DCPL0000393775

751. 7309415
NB

Irish Street Art

Stencils, Paste Ups, Murals & Portraits

Rua Meegan & Lauren Teeling

Fink
Dublin

KT-132-196

SECTIONS:

PROFILES:

INTRODUCTION

This entire project began with a conversation about the stencils, paste ups and murals we'd noticed around our area whilst going about our daily routines. What we particularly loved about the pieces was the distinctively Irish personality imbued within them. Most of all we respected their universal nature; free art for the masses that can be loved, hated or ignored.

Both the interesting and the unfortunate thing about street art is its transient nature, so we began to document what we were seeing. It was amazing just how much street art the cities and towns of Ireland revealed once we began to look for it. Although the Irish street art scene is in it's infancy in comparison to cities such as Barcelona, New York or London it does exist and has begun to grow in the last decade with the help of dedicated artists getting out there and using the streets as a medium for uncensored social commentary, political opposition and satire. Many street art books have paid homage to their respective countries and cities but this is Ireland's first.

Our endeavour with this book is to pay tribute to those artists who brave the elements, the injuries and the Gardaí to put something out there in the world; a thought, an idea or a joke that makes us laugh as we walk by. We also hope that this collection of work will encourage the creative spirit of the next generation of Irish street artists so that the scene here may continue to grow and make a name for itself among the worldwide street art community.

SOCIETY

ADW
Rathmines
Dublin 6

"Bertie was gone, but there was still something that I
wanted to say. The recession had hit, Bertie was the face
of that, he was the top dog."
ADW

Top left
Artist Unknown
Harolds Cross
Dublin 6W

Top right
Littleman
Dublin

Bottom left
Artist Unknown
Smithfield
Dublin 7

Bottom middle
Xπr
Dublin

Bottom right
Xπr
Dublin

Left
ADW
County Kildare

Right
ADW
Dame Street
Dublin 2

Canvaz & Xπr
City Quay
Dublin 2

Top
ADW
Dublin

Bottom left
ADW
Dublin

Bottom right
ADW
Pleasants Street
Dublin 8

"I am heavily influenced by modern culture and current events. Street art is like an underground newspaper, commenting on the news of the day."
Canvaz

The Nanny State
Canvaz
Sandymount
Dublin 4

The Truth Lies...

Maser
South Richmond Street
Dublin 2

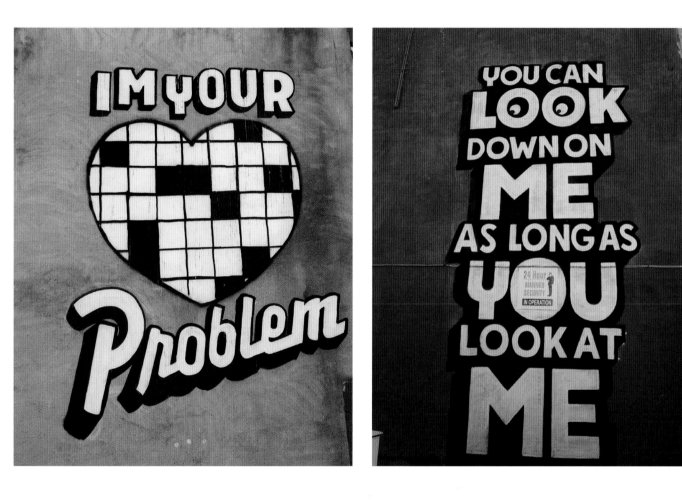

ESPO (USA)
Tivoli
Francis Street
Dublin 8

"There was originally a meaning behind littleman, something about the balance between conformity and unity, but that was soon forgotten and it turned into a massive exercise in branding. Once littleman became a familiar image it began to take on meanings all on its own." Littleman

Top left
Artist Unknown
Dublin

Top Right
Artist Unknown
Rathmines
Dublin 6

Bottom left
Littleman
Kill
County Kildare

Bottom right
Canvaz
Molesworth Street
Dublin 2

Top
Xπr
Dublin

Botton left
Asbestos
Dublin

Bottom right
ADW
Rathmines
Dublin 6

Top
ADW
Kings of Concrete '09
Dublin

Bottom
ADW
Stephen's Green
Dublin 2

"The leprechaun was a reference to the recession that I just wanted to turn into something funny. A leprechaun normally has a big pot of gold but this guy had empty pockets."

ADW

ADW
Harcourt Lane
Dublin 2

Will Saint Leger
Dame Street
Dublin 2

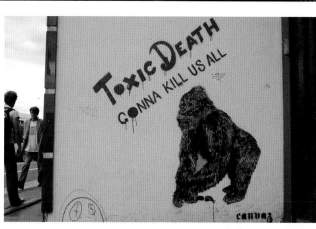

Top
Maser
East Wall
Dublin 1

Left middle
Maser
Dublin

Right middle
Canvaz
Ormond Quay
Dublin 1

Bottom
Canvaz
Temple Bar
Dublin 2

Top left
Will Saint Leger
Benburb Street
Dublin 7

Top right
Canvaz
Thomas Street
Dublin 8

Bottom
Will Saint Leger & Maser
South Richmond Street
Dublin 2

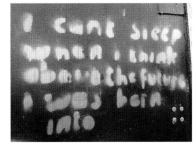

Top	Bottom left	Bottom middle	Bottom right
Canvaz	Artist Unknown	Artist Unknown	Artist Unknown
Burgh Quay	Rathgar	Rathmines	Liberty Lane
Dublin 2	Dublin 6	Dublin 6	Dublin 8

Top
Karma
IFSC
Dublin 1

Bottom left & right
Maser
Dublin

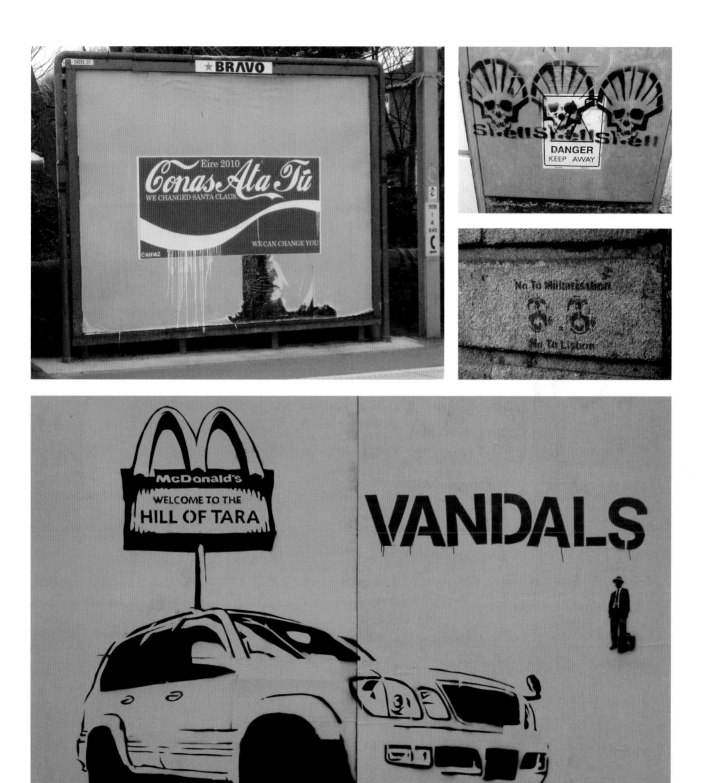

Top left
Canvas
Landsdowne Road
Dublin 4

Top right
Artist Unknown
Galway

Middle right
Artist Unknown
Dublin

Bottom
Will Saint Leger
Kings of Concrete '07
Dublin

Left
Motorman
The Bogside Artists
Derry
County Derry

Right
Petrol Bomber
The Bogside Artists
Derry
County Derry

"As kids we knew what it was like to flee from the snatch squads which is what the mural is about. It shows the human dimension of the drama. The human dimension of the troubles in Derry is really what we set out to express and that is why the murals strike a chord with so many foreign visitors. They are universal in their meaning and were meant to be so. Thus the gallery is a socialist document in essence and it amazes us that this most important point is ignored or lost on locals and easily understood by visitors."
Tom

"Charles Dicken's immortal statement that, "nothing is more keenly felt or understood than injustice by a child," sums it up for me."
William

"It captures an era and tells it like it is because kids were very much involved in the first riots."
Kevin

"The Sitting Kid, is everywhere at once.
Dublin, Belfast, Paris, but also New York,
Berlin, Rome, Beijing or Tokyo.
A silent witness of the world."
Jef Aerosol

Top & bottom right
Jef Aerosol(FRA)
Falls Road
Belfast

Bottom left
Maser &
Artist Unknown
Dublin

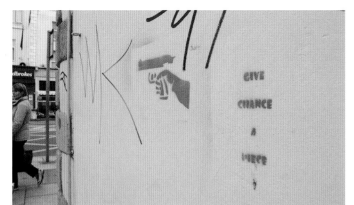

Top left
Artist Unknown
Camden Street
Dublin 2

Top right
Will Saint Leger
Dame Street
Dublin 2

Middle left
Will Saint Leger
Clanbrassil Street
Dublin 8

Bottom right
ADW
Rathmines
Dublin 6

Opposite top left
ADW
Stradbally
County Laois

Opposite top right
Canvaz
Dublin

Opposite Bottom
ADW
Rathmines
Dublin 6

"Most of my work is of recognisable characters with a funny twist to appeal to people of many ages. I want the pun of my work to be instant because more often than not people don't have time to study art on the street. Street art is something to be admired in passing. One of my first pieces was of Bin Laden. I thought it would be funny to put the world's most wanted man casually crawling into his cave, just minutes after stocking up in Tesco". Vango

Top left & right	Middle left to right	Vango	Artist Unknown	Bottom
"Dog save the queen"	Artist Unknown	Killarney	Smithfield	Vango
Dface (UK)	Tivoli	County Kerry	Dublin 7	Killarney
Dublin	Francis Street			County Kerry
	Dublin 8			

Xπr
Smithfield
Dublin 7

I WANTED A BETTER LIFE BUT I GOT WAS THIS T-SHIRT

Top left
Xπr & Gene
Pearse Street
Dublin 2

Top right
Canvaz
Heuston Station
Dublin 8

Bottom left
Canvaz
Dame Street
Dublin 2

Bottom right
Canvaz
Ballsbridge
Dublin 4

"I spotted the area for the Newton piece and the idea sprung to mind instantly. I thought of how I could use the tree already there in this piece. I decided to make clay apples and hang them from the tree to give it a 3d feel. The pun in this piece is similar to the Einstein piece. Newton, one of the world's greatest discoverers using an apple laptop to answer his questions".

"I wanted the world's smartest man unable to compete with the forever developing brain of the internet. I wanted to portray Einstein as down and out hence the bottle of Jameson". Vango

Top
Rugman (U.K)
City Quay
Dublin 2

Bottom
Vango
Killarney
County Kerry

ADW

I've always been interested in Street Art, ever since I was a kid growing up in school. At the time I was interested in graffiti and tagging. I used to draw on my copy books and on the desks but I never picked up a can and did it illegally.

A couple of years back the whole street art scene exploded in Ireland. It took off and I was just sitting back, looking at it. I used to pass by the Bernard Shaw and see the pieces outside that Maser had done. It was inspiring.

For me street art is a way for me to produce and create something, to express myself and the things that I want to say. Street art itself is a mass marketing tool. If you want to say something, you get it up in a good spot and people are going to see it. I'm inspired by everyday events. The reason several of my pieces are Irish influenced

is because they're personal to me. I put these themes up on the street for people to see, to make them smile. It's about taking the negatives we have in society, the lack of money, the trouble with the catholic church and poking fun at them.

When I go out on the streets to do a piece it's definitely an adrenaline rush. It's great when your walking away knowing you've gotten away with it and that you're happy with the piece. Sometimes it's pretty depressing when you're walking away and you know you could have done better.

If anyone is out there, producing or creating, even if it's crap in other people's eyes, as long as they're doing it, that to me is what it's all about.

INSTALLATION

In March 2007 these two paintings of An Taoiseach Brian Cowan (The Irish Prime Minister) were covertly placed on the walls of the National Gallery of Ireland and The Royal Hibernian Academy Gallery. The paintings were soon removed by gallery authorities and the Gardaí were called to investigate.

A reporter got wind of the guerilla art attacks and published the story along with pictures of the pieces in national broadsheet The Sunday Tribune. The following day the Irish state broadcaster, RTE, ran a humorously natured report on the incidents. The report was met by serious criticism from some politicians who claimed that it was of bad taste and some even called for the resignation of RTE's Director General. There was further controversy when opposition politicians claimed a breach of freedom of expression laws after RTE pulled the report from subsequent broadcasts and issued a formal apology to Brian Cowen.

The controversy continued when national radio station Today FM revealed they had been in contact with the artist and Gardaí detectives turned up at the station offices demanding information. Today FM refused to divulge any details and were then threatened with a search warrant, spurring further political reaction.

The artist, eventually revealed as Conor Casby, turned himself in to the Gardaí voluntarily. He was investigated for offending decency, incitement to hatred and criminal damage but no charges were ever brought against him.

"In the seclusion of my own home I thought that the image of Brian Cowen was ambiguous enough to stimulate conversation, funny enough to generate laughter and that the representation of the Taoiseach in situations that we all find ourselves in would draw attention to the use of images for particular reasons, rather than be seen as an image used to say something. Maybe in the latter regard I should have slimmed him down but who looks well leaning over like that? I actually based the image on my own body, albeit slightly exaggerated. In any event, such was the umbrage taken by a handful of people that it was reported to the Gardaí and they had no choice but to pursue it.

My original statement was ultimately about the control exerted by powerful people over what images appear in the media and the implicit importance of image, being as it is consciously crafted by them, and I suspect interpreted unconsciously by us. I don't think the experience had a negative effect on me at all really. And it was positive insofar as I wasn't stuck for small talk in any social occasion for the few months afterwards." Conor Casby

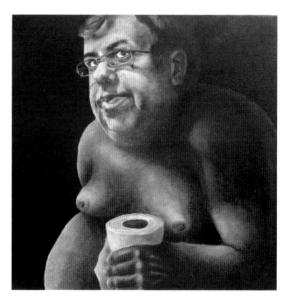

Opposite
Top
Conor Casby
Royal Hiberninan Academy Gallery
Dublin 2

Opposite
Bottom
Conor Casby
National Gallery of Ireland
Dublin 2

Above
Conor Casby
National Gallery of Ireland
Dublin 2

"January is a depressing month, even more so when it's at the beginning of a recession. Dublin City and it's people needed something to smile about again. Free Art Friday was a relatively new art movement that rapidly gained popularity around the World. Artists create a painting, sketch, sculpture or installation and leave it on the street. The piece can then be picked up by anyone and they can claim it as their own. Finders are encouraged to email the artist and tell them how and where they found it."

Will Saint Leger

Free Art Friday
Dublin

Gene
North County Dublin

"I drive by this field everyday to work,
it was screaming at me to play pool.
Every day I just wanted to play pool
in that field. Pool, pool, pool......" Gene

Pigshead
Artist Unknown
Outside a Dublin
Garda Station

Littleman
Thomas Street
Dublin 8

Artist Unknown
Camden Street
Dublin 8

Opposite top left
I Love Lamp
Dublin

Opposite top right
I Love Lamp
Kings of Concrete '10
Dublin

Opposite bottom left
I Love Lamp
Kings of Concrete '09
Dublin

Opposite bottom right
I Love Lamp,
Loki Demonseed & Asbestos
Dublin

Top left
Littleman
Dublin

Top right
Littleman
Trinity College
Dublin 2

Bottom left
Littleman
Harcourt Terrace Lane
Dublin 2

Bottom right
Littleman
Cardiff Lane
Dublin 2

"The lips started with a kiss from Melissa. Most of them are cast in plaster but there's a few in resin, crystal and bronze. I put around 600 lips in Dublin and a handful in New York. I'd say only half that number remain but it's interesting, to see which ones got removed. Sculptural street art is received very differently from paint. With 3D work you can stride around town confidently sticking pieces in high traffic areas. There's a lot less skulking around in dark alleys and avoiding the Gardaí."Littleman

"I wanted to do something to mark the International Landmine Awareness Day on the 4th of April each year. I picked the 1st of April as my planting day because if I got nicked by the cops I would use April Fool's day as a pathetic excuse for placing dozens of fake bombs around an Irish city! I bought 100 enamel plates and spray painted them army green, then me, Xπr & D$ stenciled a skull & cross bones and the words 'landmine' onto them in white. I also put a sticker underneath that gave the finder facts about the landmine issue worldwide.

The first place we planted them was Merrion Square, just across the road from the Dáil (Goverment Buildings). We then spilt up and Xπr and D$ planted some around Phoenix Park (including outside the American Ambassador's house and The President's Mansion). At lunchtime a close friend called and said that Merrion Square was closed off and crawling with cops searching the grass on their hands and knees! As it turns out an American tourist spotted a landmine' and called the emergency services!"

Will Saint Leger

Below and Opposite
Will Saint Leger
Dublin

WILL SAINT LEGER

I got into street art through activism. When I was living in London I was working with Green Peace. Stencils became one of the ways of communicating messages to the public and from there I got really interested in street art as a way to communicate ideas to people. It made sense to take what I was interested in, which was activism, and what I did well, which was art and design, and mix them together. You could stand on a street corner for hours handing out leaflets and what you're doing is educating people about an issue. But if you go and do a street piece about that issue then you present people with a different way of engaging with a subject and rather than educating them, you motivate them to do something.

RELIGION

"My Lost Angel on South William Street is one half of the piece I painted at the Cans Festival in London a few months before. Sitting with her companion beneath the tunnel in Waterloo she looks confident, watching the crowds, a regal creature with power and beauty. Her Dublin sister however looks lost and alone, taking shelter within the doorway like an injured bird unable to fly, vulnerable, a tragedy waiting to happen. As she takes refuge and waits for her strength to return, the good people of Dublin watch over her, they become her angels, keeping her safe.

Whilst I was painting her, a woman from behind me shouts, 'You can't paint that, I've seen that before, that's not yours. That's by that guy in London'. I felt a little uncomfortable as her face went a lovely shade of red when I told her I was 'that bloke from London."

Eelus

Opposite
Eelus (U.K)
South William Street
Dublin 2

Top left
Canvaz
Temple Bar
Dublin 2

Top right
Canvaz
Andrew's Lane
Dublin 2

Bottom
Canvaz
Dublin

Above
Eelus (U.K)
Tara Street
Dublin 2

ADW
St. Teresa's Carmelite Church
Johnson's Court
Dublin 2

Luca Maleonte (ITA)
Kings of Concrete '10
Dublin

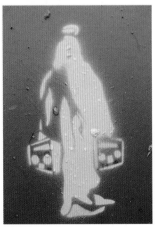

Top left
Canvas
Tivoli
Francis Street
Dublin 8

Top right
Artist Unknown
Thomas Street
Dublin 8

Bottom left to right
Artist Unknown
Cork

Artist Unknown
Cork

Canvaz
Lower Mount Street
Dublin 2

Artist Unknown
Thomas Street
Dublin 8

Artist Unknown
Tivoli
Francis Street
Dublin 8

Top left
Asbestos
Dublin

Top right
Asbestos
Dublin

Middle left
Artist Unknown
Rathmines
Dublin 6

Middle right
Canvaz
Temple Bar
Dublin 2

Below left
Asbestos
Dublin

Below right
Kong
Cork

Xπr has been painting Dublin's streets for the last decade and is an integral part of Ireland's street art community. His stencils and paste-ups are often provocative in nature and have received an abundance of media attention.

In December 2007 Xπr hit the streets with his shrouded lady stencils which comprised images of a woman whose face was covered by a headscarf. The series, inspired by the artist's sense of mischief, was designed to gauge the public's perception of such images, but the response went way beyond his expectations.

After a night out painting numerous shrouded ladies around Dublin, Xπr received a call from a friend informing him there was an article discussing the pieces in the News of the World. However, the Sunday tabloid's article was comically off the mark. The headline read "Images Of Hate; Muslim terror message". The article went on to state that "Muslim extremists have declared war on Ireland by spray painting images of hate". The journalist continued to refer to the stencils as "terrorist murals", "sinister" and "hate paintings" before stating that a prominent figure from the Irish Muslim community believes the inscription is a coded message with hidden meaning

for the terrorist group. The inscription was in fact Xπr 's tag π3.14.

In February 2007 Xπr's 'Bondage Girl' series prompted a number of newspaper articles pondering the origins and significance of the images. These works, also spurred by his mischievous nature, featured a woman whose body was bound but whose face exhibited a sense of serene calm. More recently one of Xπr's "Goodbye Kitty" pieces, which symbolises the death of the Celtic Tiger, became the featured image for the headlining article on the demise of the Irish economy in the German broadsheet 'Frankfurter Allgemeine'.

MANIFESTO

Maser
Liberty Lane
Dublin 2

don't think of all the misery
but of the beauty
that still remains

you are beautiful

DREAMS & DEDICATION
ARE A POWERFUL
COMBINATION

ARM

Passenger measure
your time,
for time is the
measure
of your being

Practice Random
Acts of Kindness

PRIVATE
CAR PARK

Every turn of
the wheel is a
revolution.

Top left
Canvaz
Anderw's Lane
Dublin 2

Middle
Artist Unknown
Dublin

Top right
Karma
Dame Street
Dublin 2

Bottom from left to right
Kong
Cork

Artist Unknown
Dublin

Artist Unknown
Belfast

From left to right
Sums
Gaetan Billault
Xπr
Will Saint Leger
Morgan
Canvaz
Maser
Fade Street
Dublin 2

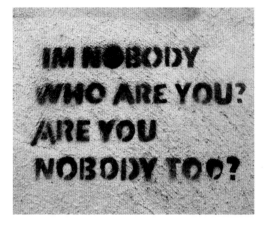

Top left
ESPO (USA)
Tivoli
Francis Street
Dublin 8

Top right
ESPO (USA)
Tivoli
Francis Street
Dublin 8

Middle
Artist Unknown
City Quay
Dublin 2

Bottom left to right
Artist Unknown
Dublin

Artist Unknown
Belfast

Artist Unknown
Andrew's Lane
Dublin 2

Top
ESPO (USA)
Tivoli
Francis Street
Dublin 8

Bottom left to right
Maser
Dublin

Artist Unknown
Cork

Artist Unknown
John Dillon Street
Dublin 8

Top
ESPO (USA)
Tivoli
Francis Street
Dublin 8

Bottom
Maser
Dublin

Left
Littleman
Hanover Quay
Dublin 2

Bottom left
Littleman
& Unknown Artist
Dublin

Right top & bottom
Littleman
Naas
County Kildare

Rugman (UK)
Moss Street
Dublin 2

Artist Unknown
Dame Lane
Dublin 2

"Uggly"
ADW
Dundrum
Dublin 16

Canvaz
Kings of Concrete '09
Dublin

Top
Karma
Andrew's Lane
Dublin 2

Bottom
Karma
Dame Court
Dublin 2

Top
Canvaz
Baggot Street
Dublin 4

Bottom
ESPO (USA)
Tivoli
Francis Street
Dublin 8

Top
Eine (UK)
George's Quay
Dublin 2

Bottom left
Maser
Dublin

Bottom right
Maser
Dublin

"Doing this was one of the most interesting nights that me and Kyja went spray painting. The cops showed up out of nowhere so we dropped our cans and ran and hid in a small bunch of bushes. The cops started shining their torches into the bushes but somehow they didn't see us. We ended up lying in those bushes in the freezing cold for about 45 minutes like two scared bitches. We had to come back a few nights later to finish it". Endo

Top
Eine (UK)
George's Quay
Moss Street
Dublin 2

Bottom
Kyja (Fra)
& Endo
Cork

Maser
South Richmond Street
Dublin 2

'They Are Us' is the name of a series of outdoor public art works inspired by Dublin city. It is a tribute to the city: Northside and Southside, the visible and the secret, the good and the bad. The work is painted by Maser and feature words by Dublin musician Damien Dempsey "With my work, I want to portray a positive message, but still address what I encounter on the street. Dublin is a central theme in my work. I spent some time traveling and painting when I was younger. The more I travelled, the more I realised how great this city is. I loved it more from being away. I chose sign-writing (as a style) because I wanted it to appeal to as many people as possible, not

just graffiti writers. I started researching Dublin sign writing from the '30s, '40s, '50s and '60s, that was an art form in itself: the typefaces they used, the leading and layouts. It's a homage to certain people like Kevin Freeney, the sign writer, who back in the 1930's, rambled through Dublin's streets on a bike or with a pushcart carrying his paints and brushes.".

The aim of the project is to raise funds to purchase a medical van to provide assistance to people affected by homelessness in Dublin City.

Interview by Barry O'Donoghue

Karma
Sandycove
County Dublin

Opposite top
Maser
Andrew's Lane
Dublin 2

Opposite middle
Maser
Liberty Lane
Dublin 8

Opposite bottom
Maser
Andrew's Lane
Dublin 2

Above
ESPO (USA)
Tivoli
Francis Street
Dublin 8

Bottom left
Kyja (Fra)
& Endo
Cork

Bottom right
ESPO (USA)
Tivoli
Francis Street
Dublin 8

MASER

Maser first started painting graffiti in Ireland in 1995 and very quickly created quite an impression on the established scene with his innovative letter styles, characters and photo realism.

Since 1995 he's treated the world as his canvas leaving behind some of his artwork in London, Austria, Germany, Copenhagen, Holland, Belgium, Prague, Slovenia, Spain and Sweden as well as making a visit to New York the birth place of his beloved art form.

Maser has also painted extensively throughout Ireland.

Maser endeavours to highlight the positive aspects of graffiti, how it can enrich the cityscape and provide an outlet for young artists. His style is reflective of this, being both uplifting and socially conscious. His work carries a message, from the simple 'Maser loves u' to the 'Love yourself today'. With this approach Maser is proclaiming to everyone his love for his city, his environment and the people that live there.
By RASK

As a self taught artist inspired by street art and street art culture, I believe in pursuing a dream.

My first piece 'Thug life' was placed in the IFSC at the height of the recession due to all those greedy corrupt bankers taking unjustified bonus packages. That kind of blatant disregard for the average joe soap was the catalyst, spurring me and my art onto the streets. I thought; If they can do that and get away with it, why can't I put up a few pieces and get away with it!

After doing my first piece I thought It was time to brighten up the streets of Dublin's great city by creating pieces with positive messages. These works were a series of three called 'city scribblers'. Each piece included a different positive message which I hoped would put a smile on someone's face or get them to think in a positive way.

Every day I spend my time trying to improve what I'm producing because I think street art is just as important or powerful as seeing a Picasso. For me, seeing a Banksy, Invader, Blek la rat or Conor Harrington (amongst others) is just as powerful, if not more so. I believe we have so many talented artists on this Island walking in the foot steps of giants but they can and will deliver. Don't fight creativity, embrace it.

A friend of mine pointed out one of my murals to his granny. She told him that she didn't care for graffiti but 'those are just nice aren't they?' That's exactly the kind of reaction I was going for. The whole point of drawing on a wall is that someone might see it and smile.

Critics and curators will always ask you for a concept, some deeper meaning that qualifies your work as art. This idea has justified a lot of almighty shite and allows little appreciation for instinctive aesthetics. Street art however, addresses the general public instead of the 'educated' elite. This means that conceptualism is validated by the work rather than the work being validated by the concept.

LOKI DEMONSEED

The work of Loki Demonseed has been described as "a world of broken hearts and families of lost children who live in the corners between Bronte and Joyce with a dash of hammer horror" Jon (Ireland's Jay-Z)

The human forms that I create have obscured identities, they the unseen, the overlooked. At times they are freaks, some with visible deformities others with emotional deformities.

There is emotional commentary wrapped in shrouds of romanticism, mystery, misery and the supernatural, the repression of what some can't even acknowledge, the limits of what you're allowed to express.

The personal narrative underlying the imagery runs deeper than the character's wounded tableau ... it is ambiguous and deliberate, working out personal emotions without having to share or define them.

My fascinations are of the dreadful nature, portraits of a tragic family; a travelling side-show, victims of their own history, they might try to eat you, but it's not their fault, its beyond their control.
Ta breantas an bhais uait!

GENE

Street art / Graffiti in Dublin has a great painting scene; totally open. For me it started with stencils thanks to a mate who introduced me to a film called "Rush" a few years ago. All nighters on the street, great sessions, and two years obsessed, I realised you can easily get bored with them as a single image, so I now try and mix them up with freehand, which is just a natural development to wherever it is I am going.

PORTRAITS

El Mac (USA)
Francis Street
Dublin 8

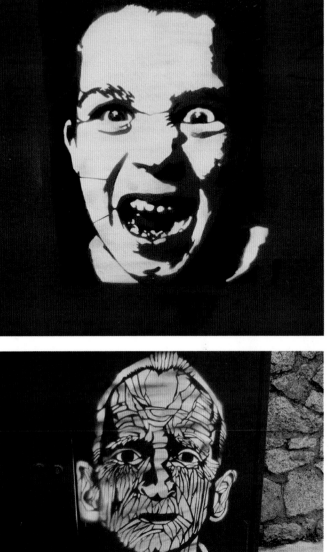

Top left
Xπr
Tivoli
Francis Street
Dublin 8

Top right
Artist Unknown
Dublin

Middle left
Artist Unknown
Eurocultured '07
Dublin

Middle right
Artist Unknown
Foxrock
Dublin 18

Bottom left
Canvaz
Dublin

Bottom right
Canvaz
Dublin

"I painted Barry for a few years. He's a friend of mine from art college. I started painting him shortly after we graduated. I wanted to engage with the ideas behind graffiti so I looked at the idea of fame. Graffiti is built on fame, that's why most writers keep writing their name over and over again. I had been also interested in identity so I took Barry as an identity and painted him as much as I could. The idea was to tag with an identity instead of a name. Thankfully Barry was ok with this so I painted him around Ireland, the UK, Spain, Italy, New York, Zimbabwe and South Africa".

Conor Harrington

Conor Harrington
Cork

Conor Harrington
Shandon
County Cork

"These two pieces aren't about a particular person but more about transience and decay. Street Artists have adapted to working in the streets, using hard-wearing materials. I wanted to take my indoor practice and literally transfer it outside so I worked on these two charcoal drawings and pasted them up on the street to see how the weather would break them down. Ireland is a great place for experimenting with rain. I think also at this stage I had been working from my studio a lot and not really engaging with the street anymore. People are always fascinated by graffiti writers lack of attachment to their pieces, you spend so long working on something and soon enough it's gone. Graffiti and Street Art has an ephemeralness that's non-existant in fine art. I thought I'd like to attach this ephemeral approach to my fine-art practice so I did these two drawings, both charcoal on paper - one of the most fragile of mediums - and put them outside to see how the outside world treats them."
Conor Harrington

Maser
Windmill Lane
Dublin 2

Top left
ZHE 155 (UK)
& K Hynes
Cork

Top middle
Gene
Bernard Shaw
South Richmond Street
Dublin 2

Top right
Xπr,
Dublin

Middle left
Artist Unknown
Kings of Concrete '09
Dublin

Middle right
Gene
Dublin

Bottom
ZHE 155 (UK)
& K Hynes
Cork

Conor Harrington
Cork

Top left
Xπr
George's Quay
Dublin 2

Bottom left to right
Xπr
Temple Bar
Dublin 2

Xπr
Dublin

Top right
Xπr
Dublin

Middle right
Xπr
Dublin

Bottom right
Xπr
Pearse Street
Dublin 2

"Samuel Beckett
was the "Frenchest"
Irish writer, so, as a
Frenchman I thought it
was interesting to paint
him in Dublin!."
Jef Aerosol (Fra)

Top left
Jef Aerosol (Fra)
Francis Street
Dublin 8

Top right
Jef Aerosol (Fra)
Drumcondra
Dublin 9

Bottom right
Jef Aerosol (Fra)
Dean Street
Dublin 8

Top left
Jef Aerosol (Fra)
Drumcondra
Dublin 9

Bottom left
Jef Aerosol (Fra)
Francis Street
Dublin 8

Right
Jef Aerosol (Fra)
Francis Street
Dublin 8

"A tribute to all
buskers, all street
artists, traditional
musicians...".
Jef Aerosol (Fra)

Top left
Asbestos
Fade Street
Dublin 2

Right top to bottom
Asbestos
Dublin

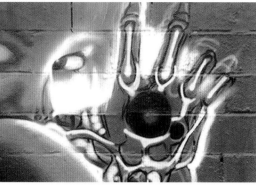

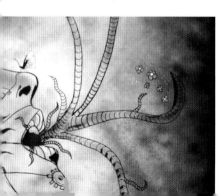

Top
ADW
Kings of Concrete '10
Dublin

Bottom
Will Saint Leger
Kings of Concrete '09
Dublin

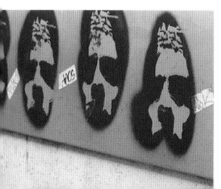  

CONOR HARRINGTON

Being a graffiti writer in Cork in the 90's was a weird experience.

There had been a flourishing scene in the late 80s and early 90s, mainly revolving around tagging, but it had all somehow almost died out by the time I got started in '94. These were the days before the internet, so getting connected was almost impossible. Your area was all you knew. I think growing up outside of a scene had instilled a sense of independence in me. There was no older writer to guide me and no pack to follow so I just ad-libbed my way through those years oblivious to all the rules and customs of graffiti.

I then went to art college in Limerick and learnt all about the history of art and other painters. It was quite a transitional period for me as I didn't know which way to go, graffiti or fine art, so it just made sense to combine them both.

CITY STREETS

Maser
Dublin

I Love Lamp
Dublin

LOST 'CLOUD'

I JUST LOOKED UP AND NOTICED MY LONELY CLOUD HAD WANDERED OFF. IT MIGHT BE NICE AND SUNNY NOW, BUT I MISS IT, SO FIND MY FLUFFY FREND AND MAIL LOST@THEARTOFASBESTOS.COM

LOST MY CORN FLAKES ARE LONELY, MY TEA WON'T LIGHTEN UP. EMAIL LOST@THEARTOFASBESTOS.COM

LOST QUIXOTIC WITHOUT THE Q, WHAT THE FUCK DOES THAT MEAN? NOTHING THATS WHAT. SO FIND MY Q AND MAIL LOST@THEARTOFASBESTOS.COM

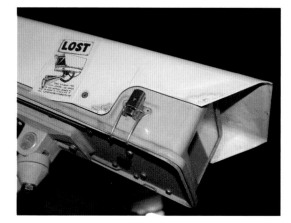

LOST REMOTE CONTROL

I'VE BEEN SICK WATCHING "WATON WISE" FOR 3 MONTHS PLEASE FREE ME FROM THIS TORTURE. IF YOU FIND IT MAIL LOST@THE-ARTOFASBESTOS.COM

Asbestos
Dublin

LOST THE MATCH

I'VE BEEN REALLY PISSED OFF SINCE WE LOST THE MATCH. HELP US GET IT BACK & MAIL LOST@THEARTOFASBESTOS.COM

LOST MARBLES

THE DAY I LOST MY MARBLES, TWO MEN IN WHITE COATS CAME TO HELP ME FIND THEM. THEY DIDN'T DO A GREAT JOB. SO IF YOU SPOT THEM MAIL LOST@THEARTOFASBESTOS.COM

LOST SNAKE

HAVE YOU SEEN THIS SNAKE? LAST SEEN BEING CHASED DOWN BY ST. PATRICK. NO SIGN OF HIM SINCE. MAIL LOST@THEARTOFASBESTOS.COM

LOST

ONE POLAROID PHOTO OF A SMALL DOG. LAST SEEN ON THE PHOTOCOPIER I COPIED THIS POSTER ON. IF FOUND PLEASE CONTACT LOST@THEARTOFASBESTOS.COM

Asbestos
Dublin

Top left	Top right	Middle left	Middle right	Bottom left	Bottom right
Will Saint Leger	Artist Unknown	Karma	Canvaz	Karma	Karma
Benburb Street	White Street	Dublin	Moss Street	Dublin	Dame Street
Dublin 7	Cork		Dublin 2		Dublin 2

Top left
Canvaz
Sandymount
Dublin 4

Top right
Fink
Sandymount
Dublin 4

Bottom left
Artist unknown
Dublin

Bottom right
Littleman
Hanover Quay
Dublin 2

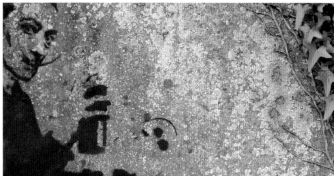

Top left	Top right	Middle right
Karma	Solus	Artist Unknown
Ranelagh	Harolds Cross	Emmet Place
Dublin 6	Dublin 6	Cork
Middle left	Bottom left	Bottom right
Artist Unknown	Fink	Endo
Cork	South Circular Road	Cork
	Dublin 8	

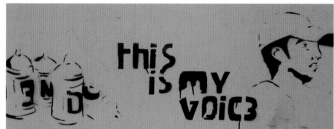

Top left	Bottom left	Middle	Right
Solus	Fink,	Karma	Dened (Hun)
Hanover Quay	Kings of Concrete '09	Hanover Quay	Kings of Concrete '09
Dublin 2	Dublin	Dublin 2	Dublin

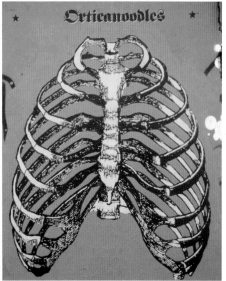

Top left
Loki Demonseed &
Splinky
Tivoli
Francis Street
Dublin 8

Middle
IamDoom
Kings of Concrete '09
Dublin

Top right
Loki Demonseed
Francis Street
Dublin 8

Middle right
Loki Demonseed
Tivoli
Francis Street
Dublin 8

Middle left
Orticanoodles
Moss Street
Dublin 2

Bottom
Lints (Den)
Tivloi
Francis Street
Dublin 8

Top
Gene
Bernard Shaw
South Richmond Street
Dublin 2

"It's just great craic to paint
something and have no idea where
you're going."
Gene

Bottom left
Loki Demonseed
Francis Street
Dublin 8

Bottom middle
Icarus Falling
Canvaz
Bishop Square
Dublin 8

Bottom right
Loki Demonseed
Tivloi
Francis Street
Dublin 8

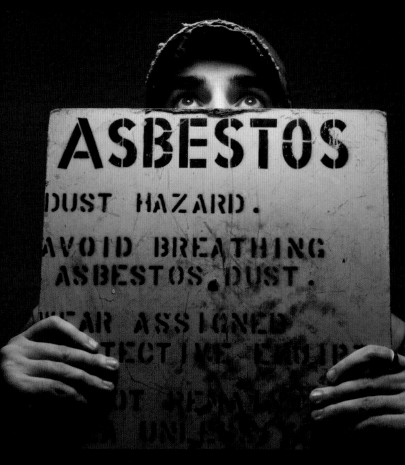

Asbestos is one of Dublin's first Street Artists and one of its best known. The alias Asbestos is based on the toxic fiber that surrounds us in the buildings of our cities that often goes unnoticed. When found, asbestos commands our attention, it is deemed to contaminate the space it occupies and evokes a serious reaction.

Asbestos began marking Dublin City with stencil projects such as his 'Jesus Saves' campaign that featured a diving Jesus figure saving a goal. These pieces were a parody on the more sincere 'Jesus Saves' scribbles that can be found all over New York city. However, on the streets he is probably best known for his "Lost" sticker series. Many thousands of stickers have been placed around Dublin requesting information on random innate objects he

claims to have lost. An email address is provided on each sticker and part of the project is judging the public's reaction by reading the feedback he receives. Messages have even been sent by a science-fiction based religious cult offering to help him find all the things he is missing from his life.

More recently Asbestos street campaigns include works combining photography, painting and the human form. The canvases for these pieces are found objects (often pieces of wood or metal) which are then reinstalled around the streets.

Cities such as Barcelona, Milan, Venice, Amsterdam, Paris, London and New York have been graced with the presence of Asbestos pieces.

FINK

I incorporate both cutting edge graffiti styles & innovative stencil based street art into my creations. My vivid use of colour & humour are key elements in my original style. My works can be seen to be influenced by Warhol, Dali, Matisse, Trans 1, Fark Fk & Jef Aerosol among others. My aim is to evoke a highly charged thought provoking sensation to the onlooker.

I LOVE LAMP

Splink was just a normal graffiti artist until one day, while helping out a friend with lighting for a film project, he was electrocuted by an antique lamp. He slowly noticed strange powers developing, but instead of super awesome Spiderman powers he got a Dr. Jekyll & Mr. Hyde style effect. Resulting

Battling with his graffiti conscience, his street art side took over, casting this lowly graffer to the curb and continuing on to put up pretty pictures of lamps all around the streets. Señor Splinky & Sir Lampsalot have now managed to get their conflicting interests under control, and along with a few more misguided misfits they have united together to form,

SPECIAL THANKS

To all the artists featured and profiled in this book for their help, trust and patience over the last two years.
A very special thanks to Jon Lynn for consistently pointing us in the right direction! To our families for their unwavering support and belief that this book would happen; Mags, Emma, Rachel, Conor, Libby, Paddy, Naoise, Leah, Thom and baby Milo. Thank you.

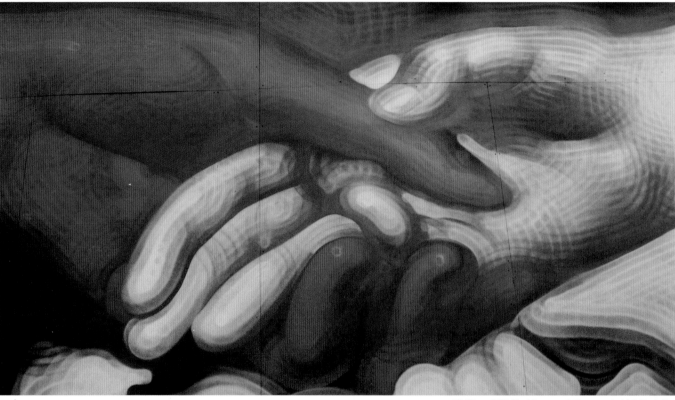

El Mac (USA), Kings of Concrete'10 Dublin

ARTIST LINKS

ADW
www.adwart.com
Will Saint Ledger
www.willstleger.com
Canvaz
www.canvazstreet.com
Maser
www.maserart.com
Karma
karmastreetart@gmail.com
Xπr
www.flickr.com/people/stencil-pi
Conor Harrington
www.conorsaysboom.wordpress.com
Loki Demonseed/ I Love Lamp
thenomnomcollective@gmail.com
Asbestos
www.theartofasbestos.com
Fink
www.flickr.com/photos/fink55
Bogside Artists
www.bogsideartists.com

INTERNATIONAL ARTIST LINKS

Eelus (UK)
www.eelus.com
Eine (UK)
www.einesigns.co.uk
Rugman (UK)
www.rugmanart.co.uk &
www.rumknuckles.com
ESPO (USA)
www.firstandfifteenth.net
Luca Molente (Ita)
www.lucamaleonte.blogspot.com
El Mac (USA)
www.elmac.net
Jef Aerosol (Fra)
www.jefaerosol.free.fr
Orticanoodles (Ita)
www.orticanoodles.com
DFace (UK)
www.dface.co.uk

ADDITIONAL PHOTOGRAPHY

Kieran Hynes
www.flickr.com/photos/kieranhynes
Mick Quinn
www.mqphoto.com
Albert Hooi
www.alberthooi.com
Aidan Kelly
www.aidan-kelly.com
Karl Martini
www.karlmartini.com
Martin Maher
www.mmphoto.ie
Richard Gilligan
www.richgilligan.com
Bláighnid McElroy
www.flickr.com/people/blaighnid
Cashen
www.flickr.com/people/cashen
Niall Carson

DESIGN AND LAYOUT

Stephen Doyle
www.stephendoyles.wordpress.com